CW00747696

PRAISE F

'Laurie Bolger's writir
a picnic, a hug and a p
weighing things" is maybe my favourite line of poetry
this year, and definitely my new life motto. Stunning.'
– Hollie McNish

'Intimate, warm, and with teeth-clenching wit, Bolger
turns the domestic into an epic. Her leaps of surreality
are breathtaking, unexpected and painful. Moving,
tender and always curious, *Makeover* is a book that will
hold your hand in the supermarket.'
– Joelle Taylor

# MAKEOVER

POEMS BY
## LAURIE BOLGER

THE EMMA PRESS

THE EMMA PRESS

First published in the UK in 2024 by The Emma Press Ltd.
Poems © Laurie Bolger 2024.

ISBN 978-1-915628-24-4

A CIP catalogue record of this book
is available from the British Library.

Cover design by Amy Louise Evans.
Edited by James Trevelyan.
Typeset by Emma Dai'an Wright.

Printed and bound in the UK by the Holodeck, Birmingham.

The Emma Press
theemmapress.com
hello@theemmapress.com
Birmingham, UK

# CONTENTS

*For Nan*

ଔ

## Peach

In the Working Men's Club they played Pennies from
Heaven / all the kids would run onto the dance floor to pick
up the coins the adults had dropped / the Working Men's
Club: with the long wall in front /

and one big tree / where people dropped in and dropped
their souls like the pennies / onto the shiny floor / how
could you want more than this /

> *it was boiling that June*
> *washing up bowls for*
> *paddling pools*
>
> *the girls made stress balls*
> *the boys made water balloons*

so the compère called the same man up to sing /

*I pulled her from her glittering packaging I wanted everything for her*
*a moth in a crush of stars        —*

Mum walks through the door in her new coat / red with
matching hat / she must be about eight or nine / and my
mum is shy / tough frown / but shy / her and Nan had to
walk through the 'men's bar' to get to the women's bit out
the back / all the men shouted / *red… alright there Little Red
Riding Hood!* /

*at night I imagined myself with the neighbour's gelled curtains*
*the boy next door who suggested a wet T-shirt contest*
*and we all lined up*

*I pulled two bits of hair down like Sporty*

I thought I told you about the committee member's wife
/ the woman who ran a snack bar where you could buy a
single sausage on a stick always for sixpence and burnt /
imagine the ballroom thick with drink / in through double
doors / Mum holding Nan's hand / holding on tight / like
she was tightroping the long wall outside / she might have
been pretending to be a film star / hand glued to hers / shell
mirror /

and later after fizzy Coke and crisps / her pushing the coins
into her small hot palm gathering them all up / *quick!* / the
coppers falling from the pockets of: Mr Ambrose / Edith
and Jean / Rita / fat peaches /
penny sweets / French chalk / women waltzing like they
were well-to-do and in love /

*I didn't learn to skateboard*
*that year I rode in the passenger seat of my cousin's dirt truck*

the first lesson in loving men until they die /
I want to twirl her / the way I twirl in the living room some
  nights /

*I let her go in the cul-de-sac*
*her plastic wings carrying her as far as the front lawn —*

Nan had her hair done in the peachy salon / the men talk
shit / and the women look lovely / *why don't you show Mary*
*your cloak? / before it gets dirty* / between pictures of boxers /
they fight at the bar /
the dusty ceiling with one balloon stuck / high heavens /
they'd need a ladder to get it down /

*I remember when Heidi's homemade stress ball exploded*
*she caught the flour in her skirt and carried it for a long time —*

# Fried Eggs

Of course I sleep on my front for three weeks before I get
measured in Marks and Spencer for two soft triangles, neat in
a box like bunting — a jolly woman gives them a letter and a
number like an order from the café next door where Mum says
*of course you can tell me anything*

        to go for flesh-coloured

  buys me an iced biscuit —
      a little girl's piped face to soften the blow.

✿

At the beach, Sam's Mum says she can't imagine Sam with any
because there's nothing of her —

Sam's Mum leaves pads on the edge of her bed
when she's at work we dye our hair red

  then shovel crisps into bright dips: Thousand Island,
    Sweet Chilli,
          Sour Cream and Salsa —

✿

Me and Sam find this book in the charity bag: *A Woman's
Guide to Man Sex*

                we practice on a big bear.

Sam's Mum finds the dips spilt down the back of the bunk bed
　　days later

sunk into every groove of the Sylvanian Families boat —
　　　　　　　　　　and the wall will need repainting now.

❀

Sam's Mum finds *A Woman's Guide to Man Sex* and can't stop
　　laughing

*what are you going to do with that, girls?*

　　　　　At swimming, she tells the other mums who we watch
in the gallery café where the glass steams up and cuts off their
　　　　　　　　　　　　　　　　　legs —

❀

When I sleep at Sam's we top-to-tail on her single bed and in
the morning Sam's Mum makes us fried eggs on thick white
bread —

we pass the ketchup and make faces on the plate.

　　　　　She talks about our weight.

❀

We clean the dried dip from the otter's plastic galley kitchen
　　it's stuck in everything.

# Mermaid

In matching swimming costumes
with go-faster frills, we lap the pool —
Mum waves at us from the sunbed.

Her husband takes a loop of the lobby,
tells the barman his life story —
helps an old lady with her bags.

Mum doesn't like getting her hair wet.
Mum points out the towel boy
with the twinkling eyes.

Someone brings chocolate eclairs;
Mum shakes her head. We say,
*but Mum, they're your favourite!*

Mum doesn't like the building work
or loud families with rude children.
Mum likes our room:

> it has a hairdryer,
> an iron,
> a safe.

I'm plastered in a football strip trying to join the stag.
I'm hanging off the banister singing something in Irish.
I'm sick in all the women's bags.

The other travellers stare when I fall.
My teeth shatter on marble —
Mum says, *oh you silly old thing* —

I wear sequins to dinner —
Mum embroiders *holiday ruined*
into the tablecloth with her eyes.

There's a tiny woman in the safe upstairs.
I tell Mum I like the towel boy's soft hair,
his twinkling eyes — I'm so hungover

my eyes fall out —
two scallops in some shells

# *Nan*

I worried about the blood in her kitchen bin
that summer I couldn't get the tampon in

                    she kept asking if I had ants in my pants
          told me I'd get fat if I kept eating crisps like that —

told us our eyes would go square
if we watched too much telly

                    told us not to pick our noses
                    because our eyes would fall out

and then there were
those real-life stories —

      a cockroach laying eggs inside a woman's tongue

We grew courgettes down the side of the garage
      mine got so big I couldn't even carry it —

          I was a big blue wet paper towel
          I was forty-ninth in the running
          I kept an alien in a plastic egg

all these
        secret things coated in gunge —
nursed at the back of the bus

and she never told Mum
        leaving her wondering
                about those men who leave the taps running —
or take the money from the ceramic chicken and spunk it —

Nan asks for a Grim Reaper Tennis Racket for Christmas
smoking    she'll let their fat bodies fry then get the hoover out

I pray her ghost will haunt the bingo hall for chips
and not be on her hands and knees scrubbing —

when me and her walk the Rec for the fiftieth time
she tells me *don't trust no one* —

says it in her sleep
before she hangs up the phone —

# The T-shirt Said

Let it Grow (a flower)

Choose You

Harmony (an undone thread)

Messy Bun & Getting it Done (a silhouette)

Choose To Shine

Planet Zen (garden and peace sign)

it said...                    No Rainy Days (just sun)

the T-shirt was cheap

Born to Sleep (some *Zzz*'s)

Positive Thinking (a full cup)

it said...

Nature Loves You Back (a ghost)

Sunshine Brigade (a bright egg)

**You do Ewe** (some sheep)

**Change is a Team Sport** (a straw)

it said...

**Live Less Worry More**

**Be the Stars** (a pill)

**Cuteness is Natural** (the sea)

it said...

**Be Brave** (a forest floor)

it said....

**Action Replay** (fire emoji)

**Lazy Sunday** (two sad phones dancing)

# Stand Together Nicely, Girls

On a stranger's front steps
you tell me to hold on
while you sort your hair out,
and to make sure I get the bridge in the background.

I feel like our Mum
when we were small,
that one of us two
stood on our front porch
in new school uniforms,
matching grey jumpers
on top of little girl vests,
or that one of us on Halloween,
you holding out a cauldron
in plastic witch's fingers,
me dressed as the Phantom of the Opera
in a bin bag and wonky mask,
or us in the pink bath
with bubbles on our heads
or matching hats at weddings
or on the top deck of ferries
all foreheads and frowns
or in my graduation gown
or matching fringes and wigs,
us two dressed as clowns,

or in the beach bar red-faced,
our hair braided like snakes,
or at the Christmas table
in our best clothes,
or you on long car journeys,
mouth open against the window.

On the plane home
I want to wake you up,
tell you that the view is magic,
                all those little lights —
rows of humans lean over
to get a photo out the window.

I take one to show you
I take one for my screensaver
I take one to show our Nan —
who's never seen the Earth from here.

# *Your Body Isn't Glamorous*

You tell me about the little girl who told you
you weren't glamorous

      I send a picture of my belly    pushed out
                    like we did
                          at West Way

                  our little Barbies on the mat

            and us pretending
        to give birth to cushions
                  on the floral couch

               Mum getting cross
*be careful not to stretch your tops like that, girls*

Perhaps she's been looking

      the same way we did

          at the all-American neon women

    and suddenly questioning
      the crisps in her lap

I've been thinking of women as houses
      how we spend whole lifetimes making do
            marrying and holding things

                  Do you remember the croissant in the tree
                        all the neighbours thought it was
                                    something
                        exotic
                        and deadly
                        when they realised it was just a pastry

      we couldn't stop laughing

I want to tell you        you are strong
that your body is glamorous
to think of all the things it can do

                  We used to put towels on our heads
                        hold daisies in our hands

do you remember

Auntie Teasy      all horoscopes and nails
          cursing and coughing
like she was emptying great bags of gravel
straight onto the coffee table

✿

I think of the little girl
          how she used the word glamorous

                    when I call you're buying peas
                          *don't worry* you tell me
                    *I've got myself a pastry for the way home.*

## Parkland Walk

Some tech god has made an app so you can hear birds and name them

the police helicopter is going so          we speak loud

the broken bird box is left hanging but they're still going

some woman told me and Hannah not to come down here on our own

*don't go down there on your own girls and if you do for god's sake stay together —*

Hannah lost her Dad last month so I was chirping at her about a place for us to get

good spaghetti

there's a snail right in the middle of things

its shiny trails are like rain caught in a spider's web

the bin has shit all over the path again

someone has graffitied a sun onto the side of the big trunks in a mess of yellow

so the bark is

like the potatoes we dipped in paint

and dragged around the plate when we were small

a jogging man is convinced that the wedding proposal is just right

and the locals have had time to draw sad faces on all of the stumps

a little girl's dad chases her along the path

I make a joke about the woman with the warning I wanted to say

*my legs are thick with blood and yes they can*                    *run*

I learnt to ride a bike on a path just like this one

I got too wide for the slide

I made perfume in milk bottles from petals for all of the mums

who told us not to go too far

I ask Hannah *what do you need, girl?* — and she says she won't remember any of this in grief

*it's like Sally said, just walk with her for now and so we walk into the trees*

# Dandelion

stubborn little thing
       so familiar with the city

never fails to push itself up
           at the side of pavements

dig deep roots
in alleyways

in the hottest of summers
       challenges the concrete —

# My body is a jar of coins from places I don't remember visiting

I'm playing hide and seek — around here the landlady has a key
we know we're her bread and butter

she's drinking Aperol on the roof with her partner that summer
I'll never forget her explaining the order of her life before this

when the fridge kicked out heat
and she bought a cream buggy and learnt the alphabet

all he wanted was a spare room with a telly no one watches
all she wanted was space

she's looking in the window at me
        walking around naming things —

these days my cash goes on weddings
a calorie counter lights up my face in the dark gym

when my body hasn't heard from itself in weeks
my smile still holds up the whole house

I can lug it in with the shopping
better than anyone —

# Watergate Bay Hotel

I ordered a sticky toffee pudding in a shiny blue bowl
let     the ice cream melt and float like petrol        took it up to the room at the top
just me and the duvet

a new sheet and my body tucked under it        and I rubbed my feet back together
and let a comedian keep me company on the little telly in the corner        and I was glad

not to have to be anywhere  or anyone's        and the sea got darker I got stiller

and I can't remember leaving the bowl or the spoon but it greeted me in the morning     sides
going hard on the grey bedside like cold sand drying in the bright —

Everyone's favourite Sunday weather        everyone out there already
when the morning knocked the door        I laid there the same way lovers do

pulling the other one back to bed as the shower calls their warm bodies in —

# *Shine*

Some women hand down bits of cloth          a decent teapot
heart-shaped things
wartime irons so heavy they could hold open the door

I've been handed wedding rings and the force to hold
                        a whole house above my head —

Mum's rings don't fit now
says her hands are as knobbly
as the trees that lined the street she first held me in —

Mum lost her favourite colander in the pub kitchen
straining the sticky sweet pineapple to go with the cheese
   on sticks —

So leave me the power in your hips

so when I think of you
I think of the sink as a lake you could dive in

and if I'm left that pie dish
I want it full of all the things they said about us
leave me the measurements of a kitchen, Mum

I want to live without weighing things —

# Swim

When my pastel-coloured swimming costume started to wear away at the chest
it told my legs to keep on swimming          to be flecks of 80s confetti and prick the man who
          called them *pins*

                    *nice pins* he kept saying from the window of the plastic barber shop
          the bus stop          the supermarket floor.

          I swam past them all
the little men

                              got stuck in the filter

like they told me I would with all my hair

          my fake glow fell away
          I swam past the prom dress on the hanger
          and through the turnstile at Loftus Road

half-finished to be told  
or that I had bedroom eyes

this time not like an animal waiting  
not to dilly dally

but to kick back

past all the perfect people in perfect towns  
who weren't perfect and nor was their town —

past the commuters who shouted *sack the juggler!*

I left them to clumsily drag themselves home plastered

and I swam past the road  
where women take their joy out with the bins  
past the chippy     and the bikes     the barman who asked me to stay

past the local who asked what my real job was as he highlighted the tv guide  
and I thought about my Mum     all those years

and her heart

a big octopus of a thing

that was inked to see what was going on with it

   and mine kept on floating

so I kept on going

      past the girls who threatened to drown me

      past the big brick they kept making us dive down for

I took off my cap

   and I swung it

      and my hair was whiter than the tiles' shine

      I climbed out      of the chlorine

the legs of the mums in the gallery café all cheered

         and I was the most upright thing —

## ACKNOWLEDGEMENTS

A huge thank you to the Nans, Mums, Gems... Daisys, Alices, Lauras, Sallys, Lilys, Sarahs, Hannahs, Erins, Marias, Hayleys, Elizas, Phoebes, Jennis, Lizzys, Claires & Máiréads... & to all of the amazing women in my community.

Thank you to James Trevelyan & the team at the Emma Press for handling my work with such care. Thanks to Amy Louise Evans for the beautiful artwork... you are amazing.

Thank you to Caroline Bird & Andrew McMillan for guiding my writing since the start. Thanks to Hollie McNish & Joelle Taylor for believing in these poems.

Finally, to the scribblers who join me online every week: you lift me up constantly.

To the women on the set of *Makeover*, you know who you are... *Makeover* is for you.

## ABOUT THE POET

Laurie Bolger is a London-based writer and founder of The Creative Writing Breakfast Club. Her debut pamphlet *Box Rooms* (Burning Eye) has featured at Glastonbury, TATE, RA & Sky Arts.

Laurie's writing has appeared in *The Poetry Review, The London Magazine, Magma, Crannog, Stand*, and *Trinity College Icarus*, and her poems and short stories have been shortlisted for The Bridport Prize, Live Canon, Winchester and Sylvia Plath Prizes.

In 2023, Laurie's poem 'Parkland Walk' was awarded The Moth Prize, judged by Louise Glück, and Highly Commended in the Forward Prize for Poetry.

Website: www.lauriebolger.com
Instagram @lauriebolger_
X @lauriebolger

## ABOUT THE EMMA PRESS

The Emma Press is an independent publishing house based in the Jewellery Quarter, Birmingham, UK. It was founded in 2012 by Emma Dai'an Wright, and specialises in poetry, short fiction and children's books.

The Emma Press has been shortlisted for the Michael Marks Award for Poetry Pamphlet Publishers in 2014, 2015, 2016, 2018, and 2020, winning in 2016.

In 2020-23 the Emma Press received funding from Arts Council England's Elevate programme, developed to enhance the diversity of the arts and cultural sector by strengthening the resilience of diverse-led organisations.

Website: theemmapress.com
Facebook, X and Instagram:
@TheEmmaPress